THOUGHT CATALOG BOOKS

More Than 20 Minutes
Of Reading

More Than 20 Minutes Of Reading

Everything You Need To Read About The Brock Turner Case And Controversy

THOUGHT CATALOG

THOUGHT CATALOG BOOKS

Brooklyn, NY

THOUGHT CATALOG BOOKS

Copyright © 2016 by The Thought & Expression Co.

All rights reserved. Published by Thought Catalog Books, a division of The Thought & Expression Co., Williamsburg, Brooklyn. Founded in 2010, Thought Catalog is a website and imprint dedicated to your ideas and stories. We publish fiction and non-fiction from emerging and established writers across all genres. For general information and submissions: manuscripts@thoughtcatalog.com.

First edition, 2016

ISBN 978-1534636248

10 9 8 7 6 5 4 3 2 1

Cover design by © KJ Parish

Contents

	Introduction	1
1.	For Brock Turner, The Rapist, From Women Who Know What He Is —*Emma Bleker*	3
2.	How In The Hell Does Brock Allen Turner Sexually Assault An Unconscious Woman And It Not Be Considered Rape? —*Hattie Weber, Senior Editor of Badass + Living*	7
3.	'Rape Isn't Always Because Of Rapists!' Brock Turner's Friend Says In His Defense —*Jacob Geers*	15
4.	Brock And Dan Turner, Please Read This —*Madison Geoghagan*	21
5.	Dear Dan Turner, You're No Kind Of Father —*Marisa Donnelly*	25
6.	15 Infuriating Quotes From Brock Turner's Statement That Show His Lack Of Accountability And The Prevalence Of Rape Culture In 2016 —*Kendra Syrdal*	29
7.	This Is The 'Steep Price' Of Rape (And It Has Nothing To Do With Brock Turner's Short Six Months In Jail) —*Cassandra Fawley*	35
8.	I Am A Victim Of Rape And This Is What I Think About The Stanford Swimmer Only Getting 6 Months For Sexual Assault —*Liza Larregui*	39

9. 13 Powerful Quotes From Vice President Joe Biden's Letter   43
To The Survivor Of Brock Turner's Attack
—*Kendra Syrdal*

10. This A Letter To The Person Who Really Matters In The   47
Brock Turner Case—The Survivor.
—*Jennifer Rodriguez*

11. Why We Owe To Ourselves As Women And Survivors To   51
Keep The Brock Turner Conversation Going
—*Abby Rosmarin*

12. 27 Quotes From The Survivor Of Brock Turner's Rape   57
That Are The Absolute Pinnacle Of Strength And Grace
—*Daniel Hayes*

Introduction

Brock Allen Turner was arrested on January 18th, 2015 outside of the Kappa Alpha fraternity at Stanford University. The reason for his arrest?

Rape.

Two PHD students biking by the fraternity saw Turner on top of an unconscious and incapacitated woman behind a dumpster. Upon noticing strange behavior (he was moving and she was not) they called out to him and when he tried to flee, chased him until they tackled him to the ground and held him down. These graduate students held Turner until police arrived where he was arrested.

In June of 2016, the formal rape charges against Turner were dropped. He was convicted of three other felony assault charges and sentenced to six months of prison and probation, grossly under the 2 year minimum for rape. Judge Perskey who delivered the sentence justified his decision stating a long sentence would have "severe impact" on Turner, who prior to the assault had been a champion swimmer.

The internet exploded over this case.

Everyone with a Twitter account and keyboard seemingly had an opinion. Turner's friends and family came out in support saying his life shouldn't be defined by 20 minutes of misjudgment. The survivor of the assault penned a 7,100-word statement that instantly went viral with its powerful words detailing the aftermath of the trauma she was subjected to. The weekend following the sentencing several letters and petitions were formed by the Stanford community asking for a more severe punishment to match the severity of Brock Allen Turner's crime.

But what does it all mean? And what do we actually need to learn?

What, when faced head-on with trauma and tragedy, should we take away from the situation?

The following essays and articles were written when Brock Turner and his case were at the forefront of the media. He was in every headline and trending everywhere. It was all anyone was talking about. It was the definition of viral. The essays investigate not only the various opinions that surrounded the case but also detail what happens when a real-life trigger warning is thrust your way.

It is not a narrative that is comfortable, but it is one that is absolutely necessary.

1
For Brock Turner, The Rapist, From Women Who Know What He Is

Emma Bleker

I want to know how you took, as a child.
When your mother told you 'no,'
did you bite at her fingers, snarl until
the spit slipped down your chin—
contort into animal, control knotted back
into swarms in your fingers.
Did they tell you how to sting, without
thinking about the purse of skin it leaves?
Did she call you her tempered little boy,
calm all the while—
were you listening with swinging smile,
pleasured, dripping jaw swung open, still,
from around the corner when your father
told her in the kitchen: 'this is just how boys are'?
When her bandaged arm held you close,
said sweet in your ear, 'none of this is your fault.'
Did your father ask why you stopped biting,
if you really wanted what was being kept from you?

Did he ask you in front of your mother,
as she cradled the place where the raw skin was wrapped up?
As she nodded along,
this was not enough.
You, 7, learn to swim.
You, finding most joy in pulling those who
cannot, by their ankles, into the
deepest end of the water.
And again, you carefree boy,
again you are forgiven. The girl you pulled
in, she wore her best dress,
which now has no use for her anymore.
It will always hold the memory
of taking on water
and threatening to drag her
further under.
Your father says she should have learned,
this would not have happened
if only she was better at knowing
how boys play. This is how men play.
You, 13, reach under the skirt of a girl
in the lunch line, grab hard like your hand
is learning how to make anything
its own. You hiss, boy, something like 'I like my
girls thick.' You leave marks where your fingernails
tried to teach her your name. Where she tried to
keep her skin her own.
You, using the word 'mine'
in honors English essays, in place of naming unconquered
places. Just places, with names you did not bother to learn.

She hears you grit your teeth next to her ear
at night, decides on jeans, the next day,
and the next. Decides to call herself 'unclaimed.'
Easier that way,
they cannot say she earned that hand,
cannot say her name sounds different, today.
This is the war you breed.
And we,
knowing the ways they will promise us,
vow to us, seep into us—
we are not worth protecting.
You, still that pillar worth protecting.
Tell us, when did you realize you could not
be touched, up there? And when,
we beg, did you understand
what that could mean? What that would mean?
You, now 20—
we know how this one sounds.
Keep speaking it until our lips crack,
until we taste ourselves bleeding,
again,
as she tasted herself
bleeding.
For you, and for your father—
did you go to see the dust
they dug out of her?
We know you.
We went to meet the dust.
We have seen that dirt,
that muck,

those twigs,
those photographs—
insides swollen, from— what did you say?
from coming too fast? coming, as she slept?
Coming, without knowing she still had skin?—
And we, we see ourselves in that
swell, in that debris carved out
of the body.
We see it every day.

2
How In The Hell Does Brock Allen Turner Sexually Assault An Unconscious Woman And It Not Be Considered Rape?

Hattie Weber, Senior Editor of Badass + Living

By now, you have almost definitely heard about Brock Allen Turner, the man convicted of three sexual assault felonies. The reason you've been seeing his name in the news and all over social media? Beyond committing a heinous and unthinkable crime where *he sexually assaulted an unconscious woman* and was convicted of three sexual assault felonies, **he's only been sentenced to six months in jail**.

Six months. Even class A misdemeanors—such as resisting arrest or possession of a controlled substance—can land you in a county jail for up to a year. But three felonies and sexually assaulting an unconscious woman and this guy gets six months and has to register as a sex offender. As you read on, you will notice that I refer to him as "Brock Allen Turner, the man convicted of three sexual assault felonies," instead of just by his name. The reason, to me, is very simple: every article I have read on this subject refers to him as a former student, or a star Stanford swimmer, or an Olympic hopeful, or something else that lessens what he actually is. **A man convicted of three sexual assault felonies.** A man who sexually assaulted an unconscious woman behind a dumpster.

I want more than anything to be able to refer to him as "rapist;" however, I cannot. Are you ready to be really pissed off? According to the state of California, he is not a rapist. In this particular state, rape is defined as "non-consensual sexual intercourse that is committed by physical force, threat of injury, or other duress." Sounds a lot like what happened, right? No. Brock Allen Turner, the man convicted of three sexual assault felonies, sexually assaulted his victim with a foreign object. This means that the *only* reason he is not a convicted rapist is because he didn't assault her with his penis. That's right, everyone. Strangers can insert foreign objects into us while we are conscious or unconscious and apparently it's not rape.

Now, before I get ahead of myself (and before I get so frustrated I just start to ramble), let me give you a bit of context in case you have been in a media blackout this week. In January of 2015, Brock Allen Turner, the man convicted of three sexual assault felonies, was found sexually assaulting an unconscious woman behind a dumpster. The woman had had too much to drink and had no recollection of leaving a party that she had attended with her younger sister. Two students on bicycles stopped to help her and prevented her attacker from fleeing the scene. Brock Allen Turner, the man convicted of three sexual assault felonies, was charged with five felonies, "one count of raping an unconscious person, one count of raping an intoxicated person, two counts of sexual penetration with a foreign object, and one count of assault while attempting to commit rape." This all would add up to about fourteen years in jail.

Before the sentencing of Brock Allen Turner, the man convicted of three sexual assault felonies, his father, Dan Turner, came to his aid, pleading with the judge to sentence him to only probation and to not make him register as a sex offender. Turner states in his letter, "[Brock's] life will never be the one that he dreamed about and worked so hard to achieve. That is a steep price to pay for 20 minutes of action out of his 20 plus years of life." **"Twenty minutes of action"** is how the father of Brock Allen Turner, the man convicted of three sexual assault felonies, refers to the sexual assault. No wonder his son thinks this behavior is OK!

I don't know about you, but my blood is boiling with anger. This is what rape culture looks like, folks.

As it stands now, Brock's life has been deeply altered forever by the events of Jan 17th and 18th. He will never be his happy go lucky self with that easy going personality and welcoming smile. His every waking minute is consumed with worry, anxiety, fear, and depression. You can see this in his face, the way he walks, his weakened voice, his lack of appetite. Brock always enjoyed certain types of food and is a very good cook himself. I was always excited to buy him a big ribeye steak to grill or to get his favorite snack for him. I had to make sure to hide some of my favorite pretzels or chips because I knew they wouldn't be around long after Brock walked in after a long swim practice. Now he barely consumes any food and eats only to exist. These verdicts have broken and shattered him and our family in so many ways. His life will never be the one that he dreamed about and worked so hard to achieve. That is a steep price to pay for 20 minutes of action out of his 20 plus years of life. The fact that he now has to register as a sexual offender for the rest of his life forever alters where he can live, visit, work, and how he will be able to interact with people and organizations. What I know as his father is that incarceration is not the appropriate punishment for Brock. He has no prior criminal history and has never been violent to anyone including his actions on the night of Jan 17th 2015. Brock can do so many positive things as a contributor to society and is totally committed to educating other college age students about the dangers of alcohol consumption and sexual promiscuity. By having people like Brock educate others on college campuses is how society can begin to break the cycle of binge drinking and its unfortunate results. Probation is the best answer for Brock in this situation and allows him to give back to society in a net positive way.

Very Respectfully,

Dan A. Turner

Here's the reality of the world that we live in: we teach our women not to be raped or sexually assaulted instead of teaching our men not to rape or sexually assault. We victims questions like 'what were your wearing?' or 'did you drink?' instead of asking the attacker 'did she/he give you consent?' and 'was she/he in the right mind to give consent?' Rape and sexual assault are something that affect both men and women, but right now I will be focusing on this one woman and this one man convicted of three sexual assault felonies. Rape culture is when a person who is convicted of sexual assault has a life that is more important than his victim's life. Rape culture is when a person is convicted of sexual assault and gets a minimum sentence because he had such a bright future and she was drunk. Rape culture is trying to ignore or devalue the trauma a victim suffered because she wasn't conscious enough to not get sexually assaulted. Rape culture is blaming the victim. Rape culture is telling the victim that even though she was unconscious she enjoyed it.

It's easy to write off the idea of rape culture as some crazy, anti-man, feminist movement, but it is a real problem and it is very evident in our society. We teach our young girls not to "ask for it." Not to dress "too slutty" or too prude like, not to wear too much make up or too little, not to drink too much but not to be a buzzkill. We teach them not to be a victim instead of teaching our men not to attack. And I know, I know, not all men are rapists and not all men will sexually assault someone; however, would you only teach a handful of kids how to read because you assume the rest will pick it up on their own? No. You teach them all to read and you teach them all not to rape or sexually assault someone. It is a cultural problem that was discussed by the *Psychology Benefits Society*. They shared three qualities of rape culture and how we can fix them within our society. The qualities listed were: hypermasculinity, sexual objectification of women's bodies, and systematic and institutional support—the last quality we can see in the case of Brock Allen Turner, the man convicted of three sexual assault felonies.

After the sentencing of her aggressor, the young woman provided a statement to BuzzFeed News. There were over two dozen quotes I pulled out wanting to share of her reaction. This woman, so genuine, honest, and brave, who put her life on hold for a year to get a sentencing, didn't want her aggressor to rot in prison. She just wanted him to understand that what he did was not acceptable. Brock Allen Turner's father, the father of the man convicted of three sexual assault felonies, and the sentencing shows us rape culture through the support of the young man's decision to assault this young woman. She addressed her aggressor through Buzzfeed, saying, "If you think I was spared, came out unscathed, that today I ride off into sunset, while you suffer the greatest blow, you are mistaken. Nobody wins… Your damage was concrete; stripped of titles, degrees, enrollment. My damage was internal, unseen, I carry it with me. You took away my worth, my privacy, my energy, my time, my safety, my intimacy, my confidence, my own voice, until today."

Rape and sexual assault are very real, very serious issues that plague our society. The National Sexual Violence Resource Center reports that "one in five women and one in seventy-one men will be raped at some point in their lives." If you or someone you know has been raped or sexually assaulted you can call the National Sexual Assault Telephone Hotline at **(800) 656-4673** and you will be connected with a confidential and judgement-free staff member who can assist you.

It takes very brave women like the one that Brock Allen Turner, the man convicted of three sexual assault felonies, assaulted to speak up. In conclusion to her statement to BuzzFeed, she addresses every woman, saying: "I hope that by speaking today, you absorbed a small amount of light, a small knowing that you can't be silenced, a small satisfaction that justice was served, a small assurance that we are getting somewhere, and a big, big knowing that you are important, unquestionably, you are untouchable, you are beautiful, you are to be valued, respected, undeniably, every minute of every day, you are powerful and nobody can take that away from you. To girls everywhere, I am with you. Thank you."

This chapter originated as an article on Badass + Living.

3
'Rape Isn't Always Because Of Rapists!' Brock Turner's Friend Says In His Defense

Jacob Geers

Brock Turner is the former Stanford swimmer who was found guilty of sexual assault and sentenced to only six months in jail because the judge thought "prison might effect him." Right before that sentence was handed down, however, he had a remarkable defender in an old friend, who penned a letter to the court.

His friend, Leslie Rasmussen, blames his conviction on "political correctness," saying that Brock isn't a rapist, he was just drunk and confused. After all, she says Brock was always very sweet to people in high school, so that makes up for it right?

But where do we draw the line and stop worrying about being politically correct every second of the day and see that rape on campuses isn't always because people are rapists.

She goes on to say that this instance, "is completely different from a woman getting kidnapped and raped as she is walking to her car." And implies that being drunk should be a feasible excuse for raping someone—among hundreds of other crimes too, I suppose.

Honorable Judge Aaron Persky,

It was with great sadness that I read the news about Brock Turner, and the horrible situation that he was involved in. It came as a huge shock to me.

Brock has been a peer of mine since elementary school, and was a very close friend of mine for a few years in high school. He dated one of my very good friends, Lydia Pocisk, around the same time. In those years, he was always very respectful of everyone. Teachers, classmates, friends, and girls, all alike. He is one of those people that no one has a problem with, and is pretty much good at everything. We all knew he'd swim in the olympics one day. His family is a very respectable family in town. I also know his older sister, Caroline. They all seem like such good kids brought up by two very cool and grounded par-

ents. *In all honesty, if I had to choose one kid I graduated with to be in the position Brock is, it would have never been him. I could name off 5 others that I wouldn't be surprised about. Brock is such a sweetheart and a very smart kid. I never once caught him harassing anyone, verbally or physically. That would have been so out of his character.*

It's pretty frustrating to see the light that people are putting him in now. It used to be "swim star" and now it's like he is the face of rape on campuses. It's such a false way to put it. I cannot believe it. I've thought a lot about it, ad from different angles. I tried to accept that maybe he did intend to harm this girl, but I just couldn't imagine that was the case. I know rape is a very sensitive subject, for everyone, and especially women. I am not backing it up or making excuses, but there is absolutely no way Brock went out that night with rape in his mind. I think he went to a party and was drinking, like almost every student at a university does, an was flirting with this girl, like he said. The woman recalls how much alcohol she drank, which was a lot. She was no doubt about to black out if not already. I'm sure she and Brock had been flirting at this party and decided to leave together. Just as they did she passes out, which after that many drinks, anyone would. At the same time, Brock, having a few too many drinks himself, is not completely in control of his emo-

tions. It doesn't take a rocket scientist to know that alcohol increases emotions and feelings. I think this is all a huge misunderstanding. I think that the biker who found him did the right thing by keeping him there in case he was attempting rape, but that after the investigation, it should have found Brock to be innocent.

Brock is not a monster. He is the furthest thing from anything like that, and I have known him much longer than the people involved in his case. I don't think it's fair to base the fate of the next ten + years of his life on the decision of a girl who doesn't remember anything but the amount she drank to press charges against him. I am not blaming her directly for this, because that isn't right. But where do we draw the line and stop worrying about being politically correct every second of the day and see that rape on campuses isn't always because people are rapists. It is because these universities market themselves as the biggest party schools in the country. They encourage drinking. I think it is disgusting and I am so sick of hearing that these young men are monsters when really, you are throwing barely 20-somethings into these camp-like university environments, supporting partying, and then your mid lis blown when things get out of hand. This is completely different from a woman getting kidnapped and raped as she is walking to her car in a parking lot. That is a rapist. These are not rapists. These are idiot boys and girls having too much to drink and not being aware of their surroundings and having clouded judgement. I'm not saying that is every case because I know there are young men that take advantage of young women and vice versa, but I know for a fact that Brock is not one of those people. He is respectful and caring, talented, and smart enough to know better.

Attached is a photo of Brock I took in high school. He has always had that huge, loving smile on his face. The caption is even d'awwww because he was always the sweetest to everyone.

I appreciate you taking your time to hear about my past with Brock and my opinion on the matter, and I hope you consider what I've said when looking into the sentencing. I would not be writing this letter if I had any doubt in my mind that he is innocent.

Thank you again,

Leslie Rasmussen

4
Brock And Dan Turner, Please Read This

Madison Geoghagan

I was seven years old when my mom taught me to "trust my gut" when it came to strangers who approached me when I was without adult supervision. I was taught how to kick, scream, and claw my way to safety should someone ever attempt to take me against my will.

I was eight years old when I was taught that my "private parts" were sacred and absolutely no one was allowed to touch me. I was given a series of possible scenarios and lines a predator may use to his advantage. I did not even know that such evil existed in the world.

I had just hit puberty and my body began to change. I was taught to wear bras and learned which clothes were and were no longer appropriate for my body type. I was taught how to conduct myself "like a lady" and given a list of dos and don'ts.

At what age was Brock taught how to conduct himself as a gentleman? When was he given a list of dos and don'ts when it came to socializing with the opposite sex? When was he taught that even a woman, at her most vulnerable state of

body and mind, was not an object to be used? When Brock went off to college, was he taught the importance of contraceptives, respect, and consent?

To Brock's father: your letter defending your son only shines a light on where Brock adopted his entitlement—YOU. Your failure in teaching your son the simple basics about being a decent human being does not explain the choice he made the night he raped an unconscious female. He knows right from wrong, does he not? Alcohol may impair judgement, but it does not override someone's internal conscience. Brock knew in the moment that he CHOSE to take what was not his to TAKE that he was wrong. **Why else would he have run away? He was guilty.** The only thing Brock did not think about was his victim. All it took was his "20 minutes of action" to invade his victim's life, rip away her sense of safety, her sense of self, her trust in men? In 20 minutes, Brock stole a piece of his victim—forever. He trespassed on her body and into her soul. In 20 minutes, Brock changed her entire life.

So when did it become the right of all men to take advantage of any woman? When she drinks? When she trusts the wrong person? Maybe it is when she dares to say "NO"—if she is even graced with the opportunity to object.

I want you to think of your wife. If she were to go to a work party and have a few too many alcoholic drinks, would it be her fault if she was to be raped by a male co-worker? What if it only took ten minutes? Would that make a difference? What if your mother had a trusted male friend who took advantage of her? Is that rape? What is your definition of *rape*? What is the meaning of *"consent"*?

Brock has no right to inform other men of the consequences of their actions when he doesn't understand and accept the consequences of his own act of raping an innocent, unconscious woman. I don't sympathize with his seemingly depressed state when he isn't the victim—he is the PERPETRATOR!

Although I (along with many others) feel that his six month sentence is much too light, I am slightly satisfied that he is at least going to jail. I would never wish sexual assault or rape on any human, but I do hope jail is where he learns all the lessons you failed to teach. I hope he has to listen to his gut, to feel the hair stand up on the back of his neck when a particularly unsavory character approaches him. I hope he learns what is it like to live like a deer in the presence of merciless lions. I hope, when his sentence has been served, that he understands the price of his actions is one that cannot ever be repaid.

5
Dear Dan Turner, You're No Kind Of Father

Marisa Donnelly

Dear Dan Turner,

I get it. You're a father and you're defending your son. You're standing by him, you're in full support of him, and you're being the man he needs, right? That's what fathers do. They love their children no matter what, they fight for them despite the obstacles. I understand. I really do. I'm lucky enough to have a father that is my guide, my shoulder, and my lifeline.

But I'll tell you one thing my father would *never* do. He would never call me blameless when I'm the one at fault. He would never stand in my defense when I'm so far from being right it's sickening.

See, Mr. Turner, this is where you went wrong—instead of being a *father*, teaching your son how to be a good man, you made him a victim in his own crime.

Sure, if we want to play dumb, we can all say that Brock is 'young,' that 'he was drunk' and that he 'didn't know any better.' That's all bullsh*t.

But the biggest bullsh*t of all is that *YOU know better.*

You are an adult man, one who brought a child into this world. One who, at the most crucial time in this child's life, should point him in the right direction, not try to use his athletic status as a defense for an irreversible crime committed on a twenty-three-year-old girl's lifeless body.

Not try to pretend, try to claim, try to write a letter in his defense when he's already been dubbed unanimously guilty.

What kind of message are you teaching him? Teaching every other 20-something male? That the world makes excuses for those with athletic ability? That if you play the 'innocent, flirty college kid card' it's no longer rape? That there's more value in having a good attorney and good defense then taking responsibility for your actions?

Who do you think you are?

I'm sorry, but you're not a father. You're a coward.

You claim that your son's life has been "deeply altered forever by the events on Jan. 17th and 18th" but I ask you this—What, exactly has been altered forever? Brock's eating habits? His demeanor? *His swimming career?*

What about the young girl who cannot sleep without a nightlight, who cannot go to work for months at a time, who is haunted by memories that she cannot even fully remember?

WHAT ABOUT THE REST OF HER LIFE?

In your letter you say your son's sentence is "A steep price to pay for 20 minutes of action out of his 20 plus years of life." *Action*. Really? You call thrusting an unconscious woman *action*? What, actions, exactly were happening by a girl who is passed out and incoherent? Let me tell you, since you seem to be a little confused. *None.*

Those '20 minutes of action' were 20 minutes of action by YOUR SON. 20 minutes of RAPE.

Look, Mr. Turner. I read your letter. And I read it again, just to make sure I was actually reading something real and not fake internet crap. I tried to put myself in your shoes, to imagine the embarrassment, the shame, the frustration, the fear. To see how you felt—that defending your son is the only option and I understand. It's not easy to be in that situation. I get that.

But assault is assault and rape is rape. And consequences are consequences, even if they change a career, or a dream. And no matter how you try to spin it, your son is wrong. And he needs to know that.

He needs to be guided by the man he looks up to.
He needs to be guided by you.

When I read your letter, I thought of my father. And I know he would never stand by and let me get away with something terrible, despite how much he loves me. In fact, it would be *because* he loves me that he'd watch me fall. *Because I was wrong.*

See that's the thing I don't understand about you, Mr. Turner, and it's a real shame.

Your son needs someone to admire, someone to guide him, someone to teach him how to treat women, how to be a good man, how to take responsibility for the life he's now destroyed.

He needs you. But it's a shame, because you're no kind of father.

6

15 Infuriating Quotes From Brock Turner's Statement That Show His Lack Of Accountability And The Prevalence Of Rape Culture In 2016

Kendra Syrdal

On June 2, 2016 Brock Allen Turner was convicted of three counts of felony sexual assault and sentenced to 6 months of jail time and probation for the 2015 rape and attack of who the press was calling Emily Doe. A week later his sentence would be reduced to just 3 months of jail time. The following are sections from his statement given to Santa Clara County Superior Court Judge Aaron Persky asking for leniency and condemning "campus drinking culture."

Not once in almost 1,000 words did Brock Turner admit that he raped Emily Doe, apologize to her, or confess that he was in the wrong.

1. On How The Actions Affected Him (Not The Victim)

"I can never go back to being the person I was before that day. I am no longer a swimmer, a student, a resident of California, or the product of the work that I put in to accomplish the goals that I set out in the first nineteen years of my life."

2. On Regretting Drinking And Partying

"During the day, I shake uncontrollably from the amount I torment myself by thinking about what has happened. I wish I had the ability to go back in time and never pick up a drink that night, let alone interact with [redacted]."

3. On Being Broken And Learning From Your "Mistakes"

"My shell and core of who I am as a person is forever broken from this. I am a changed person."

4. Where He Blames His Athleticism For The Events That Took Place

"I wish I never was good at swimming or had the opportunity

to attend Stanford, so maybe the newspapers wouldn't want to write stories about me."

5. How He Still Thinks He Will Benefit Society Outside Of Prison

"I know that if I were to be placed on probation, I would be able to be a benefit to society for the rest of my life. I want to earn a college degree in any capacity that I am capable to do so. And in accomplishing this task, I can make the people around me and society better through the example I will set."

6. Where He Blames College Culture For Not Teaching People The Consequences Of Rape

"I know I can show people who were like me the dangers of assuming what college life can be like without thinking about the consequences one would potentially have to make if one were to make the same decisions that I made."

7. Where He, Again, Blames Alcohol For Everything

"I want to show that people's lives can be destroyed by drinking and making poor decisions while doing so."

8. Where He Admits His Life Is Ruined, But Still Fails To Accept Responsibility

"One decision has the potential to change your entire life."

9. Where He Attempts To Synonymize Rape To Being Promiscuous

"I know I can impact and change people's attitudes towards the culture surrounded by binge drinking and sexual promiscuity that protrudes through what people think is at the core of being a college student."

10. Where He Says "He Didn't Mean To" To Lessen The Gravity Of The Situation

"I made a mistake, I drank too much, and my decisions hurt someone. But I never ever meant to intentionally hurt [redacted]. My poor decision making and excessive drinking hurt someone that night and I wish I could just take it all back."

11. On How This, Once Again, Affected Him (Not His Victim)

"I've lost my chance to swim in the Olympics. I've lost my ability to obtain a Stanford degree. I've lost employment opportunity, my reputation and most of all, my life."

12. How He'll Never Do It Again

"I will never put myself through an event where it will give someone the ability to question whether I really can be a betterment to society."

13. Where He Again Blames Alcohol, And Not Himself

"I want no one, male or female, to have to experience the destructive consequences of making decisions while under the influence of alcohol."

14. And Blames Alcohol Again

"I want to be a voice of reason in a time where people's attitudes and preconceived notions about partying and drinking have already been established."

15. How This Event Ruined His Night Of Fun

"I want to let young people know, as I did not, that things can go from fun to ruined in just one night."

7
This Is The 'Steep Price' Of Rape (And It Has Nothing To Do With Brock Turner's Short Six Months In Jail)

Cassandra Fawley

Take a moment to envision a moment in time—as though it was a play or a scene from a crappy movie. It's the year 2008 and there's a house party with multiple attendees. A young girl, barely nineteen, finds a bedroom where she can lay down because she drank just a little bit too much alcohol. Then someone else comes in the room and starts unbuttoning her pants. Helpless in her stupor, all she can do is attempt to scream and hope someone hears her as her entire life changes in just twenty minutes (or maybe even less).

As an investigation ensues, she may stop pressing charges because all of the invasive questions they ask force her to relive a nightmare over and over. People accuse her of lying or "twisting the truth" and eventually—although she is innocent—some perceive her as being in the wrong. I mean, how could she try to ruin his life like that?

Looking back she'll tell you that maybe she remembered it wrong, that as time passes she's been able to slowly move on. She'll say that she doesn't even remember his name—a lie—and that she can't remember what the party was even for—another lie. I promise you this, even though she has tried for years to forget, those few moments in time linger in the back of her mind. Sometimes, when she's busy and things are going well, she forgets they're there. Then she'll read something or see something and suddenly she's nineteen and all alone again.

Recently, that something was an article about the trial of Brock Turner. Brock is a former Stanford swimmer who, in January 2015, raped and assaulted a fellow student on campus. In response to a six-month prison sentence, which will most likely be lessened to three, his father claimed that it was an awfully steep sentence for twenty minutes of action. In addition, the news article claims that Brock is now an advocate for the prevention of assault on college campuses. So his good behavior lessened his sentence, but did it lessen his victims?

No, it didn't. When did being a pretentious asshole with a powerful daddy become justification for going around raping people? I'm sorry, but last time I checked it, doesn't. Six months in prison is nothing compared to the sentence his victim will pay for the rest of her life. She will never forget the name Brock Turner and, although I cannot speak directly on her behalf, I doubt she will ever feel completely safe again.

It's been seven and a half years from the night described at the beginning of this article. The girl still hesitates when she drinks too much because she realizes that even her friends can't be trusted. She still recalls what it feels like to relive a nightmare—over and over—and then be punished because she was a victim. She can recall one of the worst nights of her life, even though so much time has passed. Her attacker was never punished because she couldn't handle the dire questioning and the endless stares she received from those who surrounded her. In addition, she wonders how six months compares to the punishment she's served for being in the wrong place at the wrong time under negative circumstances. You see, I know how these things feel, because that young girl was me.

8
I Am A Victim Of Rape And This Is What I Think About The Stanford Swimmer Only Getting 6 Months For Sexual Assault

Liza Larregui

So many feels; so many emotions. Hate, anger, and shame spinning around my head as I think back on the days after my rape. I've written about this before and have told those close to me that I probably won't write about it again. Yet, here I am. The case involving RAPIST Brock Turner has invoked something inside me that can't be held down any longer.

I was young, and stupid—blah, blah. We can all make silly claims about ourselves, but here I am, BLAMING my behavior instead of that of a CRIMINAL.

"I should have known better!"

"I should have listened to my friends!"

"I SHOULD HAVE SAID NO LOUDER!"

That's my favorite recurring thought. I should have said NO louder? Really, Liza? Sometimes I disgust myself!

Here's the gist: I met a bad boy who wanted more from me than I wanted to give. After I said no to sex, he threatened me with the knife that lay in wait in his glove compartment and also with his build (he had much more bodily strength than I did.) I didn't even realize that what I had gone through was rape until I spoke to my friends who clued me in. No is no.

Did I tell authorities? My parents? No, and no. I was afraid he would kill me (turns out he killed his wife a few years ago before committing suicide), or hurt my parents.

Why does this matter? How does Brock come into this? Well, he was only handed a short sentence because "he wouldn't do well in prison" while his father wrote a letter explaining how poor Brock can't even eat steak anymore. Let me tell you why this matters: A WHITE MAN CAN'T EAT STEAK BECAUSE HE HAS THE SADS THAT HE GOT CAUGHT! Hang on while I grab a tissue to wipe my tears.

If he was a black man…

If he was a black man, not only would his mugshot have been posted almost immediately, but the media would have had every single last documentation of spilled milk released on the man as fast as you can dial 9-1-1.

If he was a black man, not only would he be imprisoned for the maximum sentence, he sure as hell wouldn't have the luxury of people writing letters on his behalf.

If he was a black man, he'd be guilty before he was even accused.

Because he's a white guy...

Because he's a white guy, he has the privilege of getting a soft 6 months; white guys can't handle prison like people of other races, obviously.

Because he's a white guy, there's probably a lot of doubt in the minds of those close to him of his guilt; poor, richie-rich Brock, being accused of rape, would *never* do such a thing.

What happened to the victim? I don't know her personally, but speaking from experience, unlike Brock, she will suffer a **LIFE SENTENCE:** Post Traumatic Stress Disorder, depression, anxiety. These feelings of betrayal, humiliation, shame, and fear don't just go away because a judge snapped his fingers.

We need to stop victim blaming. We need to stop encouraging girls to think they have control over someone else's actions and that we should be embarrassed because another human being hurt us.

We need to start to teaching our boys that no is NO. We need to start keeping these discussions active. We can't just talk about it when it happens then let it disappear into the never-ending 24-hour news cycle abyss.

It'll keep happening if we push these tales of human failure aside. It'll keep happening if we don't start speaking up for those who don't have a voice; those who were hurt so badly they can't process what happened. Let's end life sentences for victims, and start life sentences for criminals.

9
13 Powerful Quotes From Vice President Joe Biden's Letter To The Survivor Of Brock Turner's Attack

Kendra Syrdal

Prior to the shocking sentencing of Brock Turner for the January, 2015 rape of Emily Doe, the survivor penned a statement to read in court and then published it on the media site Buzzfeed. Following the viral reaction to the letter, hundreds of thousands of people came out in support of Emily Doe and against Brock Turner.

Vice President Joe Biden was one.

In an open letter, again published on Buzzfeed News, Vice President Biden speaks out against rape culture and not only how he stands with Emily Doe, but with women everywhere.

1. How Important But Haunting Her Statement Is/Was To Read

"[These are] Words that should be required reading for men and women of all ages.?? Words that I wish with all of my heart you never had to write."

2. How At The Core We Need To Do Better To Protect Women

"I am filled with furious anger—both that this happened to you and that our culture is still so broken that you were ever put in the position of defending your own worth."

3. On The Bravery It Took To Write And Read Her Statement

"You are a warrior—with a solid steel spine."

4. On Exactly What Rape Culture Is

"Anyone at that party who saw that you were incapacitated yet looked the other way and did not offer assistance. Anyone who dismissed what happened to you as 'just another crazy night.' Anyone who asked 'what did you expect would happen when you drank that much?' or thought you must have brought it on yourself."

5. On How Stanford And Our Society Failed Her

"You were failed by a culture on our college campuses where one in five women is sexually assaulted—year after year after year."

6. On The Terrifying Reality Of Rape In 2016

"The statistics on college sexual assault haven't gone down in the past two decades. It's obscene, and it's a failure that lies at all our feet."

7. On The Very Simple Definition Of Rape

"Sex without consent is rape. Period. It is a crime."

8. On The Men Who Stopped Turner, And The Truth Behind Being A Bystander

"Those two men epitomize what it means to be a responsible bystander. ??To do otherwise—to see an assault about to take place and do nothing to intervene—makes you part of the problem."

9. On How We All Owe It To Ourselves And Society To Do Better

"We all have a responsibility to stop the scourge of violence against women once and for all."

10. Saying Exactly What Victims And Survivors Need To Hear

"I join your global chorus of supporters because we can never say enough to survivors: I believe you. It is not your fault."

11. On Changing The Victim-Blaming Society We Live In

"We will speak to change the culture on our college campuses—a culture that continues to ask the wrong questions: *What were you wearing? ??Why were you there? What did you say? How much did you drink?* ??Instead of asking: *Why did he think he had license to rape?*"

12. On The Truth Behind Emily Doe's Bravery

"Your story has already changed lives.?? You have helped change the culture."

13. On The Power Of Speaking Out

"The millions who have been touched by your story will never forget you."

10
This A Letter To The Person Who Really Matters In The Brock Turner Case—The Survivor.

Jennifer Rodriguez

You are brave, you are smart, and you are a hero. I don't know you, but I know that you have given a voice to the thousands of women that have been assaulted.

You went to a party with the intention of simply having a good time with your sister. You went to a party just like most girls in their 20s do. You went to a party with no intention of being raped. Yet, you were painted as someone that had too much to drink and consented to being sexually assaulted.

You fell into the wrong hands that night and then were made to look like the bad guy.

Why is it that when a woman is assaulted, people feel the

need to ask, "What was she wearing? Was she drinking? Why was she partying?"

It does not matter what the woman was wearing or how much she was drinking. The problem with today's world is how we put all of the focus on the women and what she did "wrong." How about we start focusing on the men and holding them accountable for their actions. Let's teach men not to rape. Sounds stupid doesn't it? Just like it sounds stupid to tell a woman how she should act so she doesn't get assaulted. Let's teach men that it's not okay to take advantage of a woman that is in no condition to give consent.

Brock Turner could have chosen to do the right thing that night. He could have chosen to take you home or help you find your sister. Instead, he took it upon himself to violate you just because he could. No one gave him that right.

Brock Turner must have learned how to be a shitty human being from his father. After the ruling, Turner's dad, Dan, said that "20 minutes of action" have ruined his son's life.

To say that this comment infuriated me is an understatement. What about your life? Those 20 minutes forever impacted you and your family.

The rotten apple doesn't fall far from the rotten tree. Dan Turner's comments show how neither he nor his son respect women. His comments make it seem like his son has done nothing wrong and that it is okay to rape a woman. I'm absolutely positive that he would be singing a different tune if this had happened to his wife, his sister, or his daughter.

You are a survivor. Your decision to speak out is one of the most courageous things I have ever seen anyone do. I don't know you, but I stand by you. You are so brave and your words have made a difference. You have shown that speaking out is important and that words can make one hell of a difference.

11
Why We Owe To Ourselves As Women and Survivors To Keep The Brock Turner Conversation Going

Abby Rosmarin

I've already written about this before. About my own incident and how I downplayed it for years. How it took my visceral reaction to the Steubenville Rape case in 2012 to realize that I was no longer able to shrug my shoulders and label it a dumb, drunken mistake. That I might've gone off and still dated and had fun after The Incident, but it had affected me.

Remember that case? Steubenville, Ohio. What frightening parallels to Stanford. A young girl, unconscious and assaulted, and a town that was more concerned about the futures of their precious athletes. Did the newspapers talk about the football players' touchdowns or game wins? I can't remember. To be honest, I don't want to.

In many ways, my situation was considerably tamer. Tamer

than Steubenville or Stanford, tamer than what a lot of my friends had already gone through. It was one of the reasons why I downplayed it when it happened. It was also in 2005 which hosted a completely different cultural mindset than the one we have now. The idea of seeing an unconscious girl and laying on top of her was not seen as that big of a deal. Especially if it wasn't real sex (cue Whoopi Goldberg's "rape-rape" line). That's just how it was. **Are you a female who is incapacitated in some way? Better be ready to assaulted—er, I mean, "taken advantage of."**

But the few times I toed away from the narrative that it was just a drunken mistake—that it was no big deal—other things kept me from really doing anything. I could hear the hypothetical defense rip my character to shreds. I could see the hyper-focus on underage drinking (I was 19 at the time). The hyper-focus on the fact that I still talked to him online for a few months after, even as my friends yelled at me for doing that (even as I felt cold and slimy for even the tiniest online interactions). I could see my past and my personality and how I behaved afterwards getting dragged out.

And after I saw the questions that the defense asked the Stanford victim during her trial, it was just that easier to imagine how something on my end would've gone.

Do you have a history of drinking?
Do you have a drinking problem?
Do you know it's illegal to drink under the age of 21?
Why did you drink, then?

How many of your guy friends have you been physically intimate with?
How many guys have you been physically intimate with?
Were you ever drunk during those interactions?

How many guys have you fooled around with in college?
Were you dating any of them?
Did you sleep with any of them?

Are you lying?

You've known the defendant since junior high. Would you say you were close?
Close enough to experiment with being romantic?
Is this just a case of buyer's remorse?

Why did you still talk to him after the incident? Clearly you didn't feel it was a problem at the time if you still talked with him.

See, my situation was ripe for character assassination. Yes, someone pulled him off me, berating him, telling him that he knew better, but then the party went on. I'd eventually be a little more aware and then spend the night in my friend's bathroom, puking, crying, bemoaning the situation, but wording it to sound like I had some part of it—like, because I couldn't push him off me, I must've wanted it, I must've initiated it, and I was just as much to blame for it. Any friend who cared more for the guy than for me could've used those words against me.

I wasn't behind a dumpster and my assailant didn't run from two witnesses. I wasn't being dragged from party to party and had pictures taken. I would still have all my clothes on. And, again, it was 2005, where "kissing and getting frisky" with an unconscious drunk girl was part and parcel of the college experience. Don't want it? Don't drink. Too bad on you, lady. This is just the way things are.

And so I woke up the next morning in 2005, labeling the night as a lesson in knowing your limits, went home, cried in the shower, and went about my day. Went about my life. Shrugged my shoulders over The Incident and downplayed it on a conscious and unconscious level.

I'd watch his story change as friends stepped up for me—my friends confronting him, because I certainly wasn't going to. He first said that I wasn't drunk. Then he said that we were both drunk. Then he said he could've done more. Like: gold star for not "rape-rape"ing. Eventually it would all be dropped—including any interactions with him—and that was seemingly the end of that.

Life would go on. I'd dismiss it, call it The Incident, date and fool around and drink and still forget my limits from time to time. I'd eventually get married and move to another state and plan out my future. Then 2012 would hit and Steubenville would become a household name and I'd spiral out in anxiety and dread and stress and realize that I was seeing myself in those pixelated pictures—that I was hearing what celebrities and the public were saying as if it were directed towards me.

Then 2016 would hit and I would be reminded why I didn't say anything 10 years ago. A case that lacked any ambiguity, especially in this day and age, where we're finally dropping that narrative of girls "asking for it" and guys not being able to help themselves. A case that still found a way to attack the victim's character, to exalt the perpetrator's athletic merits, to spin it as a "no big deal" type of situation.

A few months of jail. No big deal. He's no threat. He's got a bright future ahead of him. Please, someone think of the guy here, and his happy-go-lucky personality. We can't ruin his life over something so trivial.

And that's where I feel the fevered need to drag up my story again. My Incident. The fact that the judge and the father and a loud minority of people echo that "no big deal" sentiment—echo many of the things I said to myself about my own situation, echoed the things I feared I would hear if I ever wanted to press charges.

Because it is a big deal. All of it.

And the last thing any of us should do is shrug our shoulders and downplay whatever it is we automatically want to downplay. We have to keep the discussion going. We have to distance ourselves as far away from that attitude in 2005 as possible – especially since we're realizing that it still exists in 2016.

12

27 Quotes From The Survivor Of Brock Turner's Rape That Are The Absolute Pinnacle Of Strength And Grace

Daniel Hayes

On June 3rd, the victim of Brock Turner's rape made her statement to the California Judge who eventually handed Turner a mere six-month sentence for rape. The statement is potent and the voice is strong and unwavering.

1. Regarding The Realization Of Her Assault At The Hospital

"When I was finally allowed to use the restroom, I pulled down the hospital pants they had given me, went to pull down my underwear, and felt nothing. I still remember the feeling of my hands touching my skin and grabbing nothing. I looked down and there was nothing. The thin piece of fabric, the only thing between my vagina and anything else, was missing and everything inside me was silenced."

2. On The Process Of Gathering Evidence And The Trauma Of Removing The Debris From Her Hair

On The Process Of Gathering Evidence And The Trauma Of Removing The Debris From Her Hair

"The three of us worked to comb the pine needles out of my hair, six hands to fill one paper bag. To calm me down, they said it's just the flora and fauna, flora and fauna. I had multiple swabs inserted into my vagina and anus, needles for shots, pills, had a nikon pointed right into my spread legs. I had long, pointed beaks inside me and had my vagina smeared with cold, blue paint to check for abrasions."

3. On The Uncertainty Of Her Entire World Shifting Under Her Feet

"On that morning, all that I was told was that I had been found behind a dumpster, potentially penetrated by a stranger, and that I should get retested for HIV because results don't always show up immediately. But for now, I should go home and get back to my normal life. Imagine stepping back into the world with only that information."

4. On The Shame, Unwarranted, Of Facing The Ones She Loves

"My boyfriend did not know what happened, but called that day and said, "I was really worried about you last night, you scared me, did you make it home okay?" I was horrified. That's when I learned I had called him that night in my blackout, left an incomprehensible voicemail, that we had also spoken on the phone, but I was slurring so heavily he was scared for me, that he repeatedly told me to go find my sister. Again, he asked me, 'What happened last night? Did you make it home okay?' I said yes, and hung up to cry."

5. On Finding Out Along With The Entire World

"One day, I was at work, scrolling through the news on my phone, and came across an article. In it, I read and learned for the first time about how I was found unconscious, with my hair disheveled, long necklace wrapped around my neck, bra pulled out of my dress, dress pulled off over my shoulders and pulled up above my waist, that I was butt naked all the way down to my boots, legs spread apart, and had been penetrated by a foreign object by someone I did not recognize. This was how I learned what happened to me, sitting at my desk reading the news at work."

6. They Reported His Swim Times

"At the bottom of the article, after I learned about the graphic details of my own sexual assault, the article listed his swimming times. She was found breathing, unresponsive with her underwear six inches away from her bare stomach curled in fetal position. By the way, he's really good at swimming. Throw in my mile time if that's what we're doing. I'm good at cooking, put that in there, I think the end is where you list your extra-curriculars to cancel out all the sickening things that've happened."

7. It Would Have Just Happened To Someone Else

"He admitted to kissing other girls at that party, one of whom was my own sister who pushed him away. He admitted to wanting to hook up with someone. I was the wounded antelope of the herd, completely alone and vulnerable, physically unable to fend for myself, and he chose me. Sometimes I think, if I hadn't gone, then this never would've happened. But then I realized, it would have happened, just to somebody else."

8. He Said He Thought I Liked It

"The night after it happened, he said he thought I liked it because I rubbed his back. A back rub.

Never mentioned me voicing consent, never mentioned us speaking, a back rub."

9. Fighting For A Year

"I was not only told that I was assaulted, I was told that

because I couldn't remember, I technically could not prove it was unwanted. And that distorted me, damaged me, almost broke me. It is the saddest type of confusion to be told I was assaulted and nearly raped, blatantly out in the open, but we don't know if it counts as assault yet. I had to fight for an entire year to make it clear that there was something wrong with this situation."

10. On The Trauma Of The Trial

"Instead of his attorney saying, Did you notice any abrasions? He said, You didn't notice any abrasions, right? This was a game of strategy, as if I could be tricked out of my own worth. The sexual assault had been so clear, but instead, here I was at the trial, answering question like:

How old are you? How much do you weigh? What did you eat that day? Well what did you have for dinner? Who made dinner? Did you drink with dinner? No, not even water? When did you drink? How much did you drink? What container did you drink out of? Who gave you the drink?"

11. More Attorney Questions

"How much do you usually drink? Who dropped you off at this party? At what time? But where exactly? What were you wearing? Why were you going to this party? What' d you do when you got there? Are you sure you did that? But what time did you do that? What does this text mean?

Who were you texting? When did you urinate? Where did you urinate? With whom did you urinate outside? Was your phone on silent when your sister called? Do you remember silencing it? Really because on page 53 I'd like to point out that you said it was set to ring."

12. Then Brock Changed His Story

"And then it came time for him to testify. This is where I became re-victimized. I want to remind you, the night after it happened he said he never planned to take me back to his dorm. He said he didn't know why we were behind a dumpster. He got up to leave because he wasn't feeling well when he was suddenly chased and attacked. Then he learned I could not remember.

So one year later, as predicted, a new dialogue emerged. Brock had a strange new story, almost sounded like a poorly written young adult novel with kissing and dancing and hand holding and lovingly tumbling onto the ground, and most importantly in this new story, there was suddenly consent. One year after the incident, he remembered, oh yeah, by the way she actually said yes, to everything, so."

13. His Every Action Violated Common Decency

"…if you are confused about whether a girl can consent, see if she can speak an entire sentence. You couldn't even do that. Just one coherent string of words. If she can't do that, then no. Don't touch her, just no. Not maybe, just no. Where was the confusion? This is common sense, human decency.

According to him, the only reason we were on the ground was because I fell down. Note; if a girl falls help her get back up. If she is too drunk to even walk and falls, do not mount her, hump her, take off her underwear, and insert your hand inside her vagina. If a girl falls help her up. If she is wearing a cardigan over her dress don't take it off so that you can touch her breasts. Maybe she is cold, maybe that's why she wore the cardigan. If her bare ass and legs are rubbing the pinecones and needles, while the weight of you pushes into her, get off her."

14. And Then Brock Ran

"You ran because you said you felt scared. I argue that you were scared because you'd be caught, not because you were scared of two terrifying Swedish grad students. The idea that you thought you were being attacked out of the blue was ludicrous. That it had nothing to do with you being on top my unconscious body. You were caught red handed, with no explanation. When they tackled you why didn't you say, 'Stop!

Everything's okay, go ask her, she's right over there, she'll tell you.' I mean you had just asked for my consent, right? I was awake, right? When the policeman arrived and interviewed the evil Swede who tackled you, he was crying so hard he couldn't speak because of what he'd seen.

Also, if you really did think they were dangerous, you just abandoned a half-naked girl to run and save yourself. No matter which way you frame it, it doesn't make sense."

15. Consent Isn't The Absence Of "No"

"'At no time did I see that she was not responding. If at any time I thought she was not responding, I would have stopped immediately.' Here's the thing; if your plan was to stop only when I was literally unresponsive, then you still do not understand. You didn't even stop when I was unconscious anyway! Someone else stopped you."

16. And It Traumatized Her Family, As Well

"My family had to see pictures of my head strapped to a gurney full of pine needles, of my body in the dirt with my eyes closed, dress hiked up, limbs limp in the dark. And then even after that, my family had to listen to your attorney say, the pictures were after the fact, we can dismiss them."

17. And They Said She Was Asking For It

"To listen him attempt to paint of a picture of me, the seductive party animal, as if somehow that would make it so that I had this coming for me. To listen to him say I sounded drunk on the phone because I'm silly and that's my goofy way of speaking. To point out that in the voicemail, I said I would reward my boyfriend and we all know what I was thinking. I assure you my rewards program is non-transferable, especially to any nameless man that approaches me."

18. This Was No "Accident" And No "Poor Decision"

"Assault is not an accident. This is not a story of another drunk college hookup with poor decision making."

19. Drinking Too Much Is Not A Crime, Assault Is

"Alcohol is not an excuse. Is it a factor? Yes. But alcohol was not the one who stripped me, fingered me, had my head dragging against the ground, with me almost fully naked. Having too much to drink was an amateur mistake that I admit to, but it is not criminal.

You were wrong for doing what nobody else was doing, which was pushing your erect dick in your pants against my naked, defenseless body concealed in a dark area, where partygoers could no longer see or protect me, and own my sister could not find me."

20. True Respect For Women Isn't Destroyed By Alcohol

"You realize, having a drinking problem is different than drinking and then forcefully trying to have sex with someone? Show men how to respect women, not how to drink less."

21. Two Lives Ruined

"I want to show people that one night of drinking can ruin two lives. You and me. You are the cause, I am the effect. You have dragged me through this hell with you, dipped me back into that night again and again. You knocked down both our towers, I collapsed at the same time you did. Your damage was concrete; stripped of titles, degrees, enrollment. My damage was internal, unseen, I carry it with me. You took away my worth, my privacy, my energy, my time, my safety, my intimacy, my confidence, my own voice, until today."

22. And The Trauma Continues

"I can't sleep alone at night without having a light on, like a five year old, because I have nightmares of being touched where I cannot wake up, I did this thing where I waited until the sun came up and I felt safe enough to sleep. For three months, I went to bed at six o'clock in the morning.

I used to pride myself on my independence, now I am afraid to go on walks in the evening, to attend social events with drinking among friends where I should be comfortable being. I have become a little barnacle always needing to be at someone's side, to have my boyfriend standing next to me, sleeping beside me, protecting me. It is embarrassing how feeble I feel, how timidly I move through life, always guarded, ready to defend myself, ready to be angry."

23. I Do Not Forgive You

"I want to say this. All the crying, the hurting you have imposed on me, I can take it. But when I see my younger sister hurting, when she is unable to keep up in school, when she is deprived of joy, when she is not sleeping, when she is crying so hard on the phone she is barely breathing, telling me over and over she is sorry for leaving me alone that night, sorry sorry sorry, when she feels more guilt than you, then I do not forgive you."

24. Immeasurable Grace

"Your life is not over, you have decades of years ahead to rewrite your story. The world is huge, it is so much bigger than Palo Alto and Stanford, and you will make a space for yourself in it where you can be useful and happy. Right now your name is tainted, so I challenge you to make a new name for yourself, to do something so good for the world, it blows everyone away. You have a brain and a voice and a heart. Use them wisely. You possess immense love from your family. That alone can pull you out of anything. Mine has held me up through all of this. Yours will hold you and you will go on.

I believe, that one day, you will understand all of this better. I hope you will become a better more honest person who can properly use this story to prevent another story like this from ever happening again. I fully support your journey to healing, to rebuilding your life, because that is the only way you'll begin to help others."

25. Old Enough To Know Better

"The probation officer factored in that the defendant is youthful and has no prior convictions. In my opinion, he is old enough to know what he did was wrong. When you are eighteen in this country you can go to war. When you are nineteen, you are old enough to pay the consequences for attempting to rape someone. He is young, but he is old enough to know better."

26. And Selfless Thankfulness

"...I want to say thank you. To everyone from the intern who made me oatmeal when I woke up at the hospital that morning, to the deputy who waited beside me, to the nurses who calmed me, to the detective who listened to me and never judged me, to my advocates who stood unwaveringly beside me, to my therapist who taught me to find courage in vulnerability, to my boss for being kind and understanding, to my incredible parents who teach me how to turn pain into strength, to my friends who remind me how to be happy, to my boyfriend who is patient and loving, to my unconquerable sister who is the other half of my heart, to Alaleh, my idol, who fought tirelessly and never doubted me. Thank you to everyone involved in the trial for their time and attention. Thank you to girls across the nation that wrote cards to my DA to give to me, so many strangers who cared for me."

27. I Am With You

"…to girls everywhere, I am with you. On nights when you feel alone, I am with you.

When people doubt you or dismiss you, I am with you. I fought everyday for you. So never stop fighting, I believe you. Lighthouses don't go running all over an island looking for boats to save; they just stand there shining. Although I can't save every boat, I hope that by speaking today, you absorbed a small amount of light, a small knowing that you can't be silenced, a small satisfaction that justice was served, a small assurance that we are getting somewhere, and a big, big knowing that you are important, unquestionably, you are untouchable, you are beautiful, you are to be valued, respected, undeniably, every minute of every day, you are powerful and nobody can take that away from you. To girls everywhere, I am with you."

Thought Catalog, it's a website.
www.thoughtcatalog.com

Social
facebook.com/thoughtcatalog
twitter.com/thoughtcatalog
tumblr.com/thoughtcatalog
instagram.com/thoughtcatalog

Corporate
www.thought.is